This journal belongs to:

_____

_____

_____

_____

Date:

Verse:

Thoughts & Notes:

Prayer Requests:

Date:

Verse:

Thoughts & Notes:

Prayer Requests:

Date:

Verse:

Thoughts & Notes:

Prayer Requests:

Date:

Verse:

Thoughts & Notes:

Prayer Requests:

Date:

Verse:

Thoughts & Notes:

Prayer Requests:

Date:

Verse:

Thoughts & Notes:

Prayer Requests:

Date:

Verse:

Thoughts & Notes:

Prayer Requests:

Date:

Verse:

Thoughts & Notes:

Prayer Requests:

Date:

Verse:

Thoughts & Notes:

Prayer Requests:

Date:

Verse:

Thoughts & Notes:

Prayer Requests:

Date:

Verse:

Thoughts & Notes:

Prayer Requests:

Date:

Verse:

Thoughts & Notes:

Prayer Requests:

Date:

Verse:

Thoughts & Notes:

Prayer Requests:

Date:

Verse:

Thoughts & Notes:

Prayer Requests:

Date:

Verse:

Thoughts & Notes:

Prayer Requests:

Date:

Verse:

Thoughts & Notes:

Prayer Requests:

Date:

Verse:

Thoughts & Notes:

Prayer Requests:

Date:

Verse:

Thoughts & Notes:

Prayer Requests:

Date:

Verse:

Thoughts & Notes:

Prayer Requests:

Date:

Verse:

Thoughts & Notes:

Prayer Requests:

Date:

Verse:

Thoughts & Notes:

Prayer Requests:

Date:

Verse:

Thoughts & Notes:

Prayer Requests:

Date:

Verse:

Thoughts & Notes:

Prayer Requests:

Date:

Verse:

Thoughts & Notes:

Prayer Requests:

Date:

Verse:

Thoughts & Notes:

Prayer Requests:

Date:

Verse:

Thoughts & Notes:

Prayer Requests:

Date:

Verse:

Thoughts & Notes:

Prayer Requests:

Date:

Verse:

Thoughts & Notes:

Prayer Requests:

Date:

Verse:

Thoughts & Notes:

Prayer Requests:

Date:

Verse:

Thoughts & Notes:

Prayer Requests:

Date:

Verse:

Thoughts & Notes:

Prayer Requests:

Date:

Verse:

Thoughts & Notes:

Prayer Requests:

Date:

Verse:

Thoughts & Notes:

Prayer Requests:

Date:

Verse:

Thoughts & Notes:

Prayer Requests:

Date:

Verse:

Thoughts & Notes:

Prayer Requests:

Date:

Verse:

Thoughts & Notes:

Prayer Requests:

Date:

Verse:

Thoughts & Notes:

Prayer Requests:

Date:

Verse:

Thoughts & Notes:

Prayer Requests:

Date:

Verse:

Thoughts & Notes:

Prayer Requests:

Date:

Verse:

Thoughts & Notes:

Prayer Requests:

Date:

Verse:

Thoughts & Notes:

Prayer Requests:

Date:

Verse:

Thoughts & Notes:

Prayer Requests:

Date:

Verse:

Thoughts & Notes:

Prayer Requests:

Date:

Verse:

Thoughts & Notes:

Prayer Requests:

Date:

Verse:

Thoughts & Notes:

Prayer Requests:

Date:

Verse:

Thoughts & Notes:

Prayer Requests:

Date:

Verse:

Thoughts & Notes:

Prayer Requests:

Date:

Verse:

Thoughts & Notes:

Prayer Requests:

Date:

Verse:

Thoughts & Notes:

Prayer Requests:

Date:

Verse:

Thoughts & Notes:

Prayer Requests:

Date:

Verse:

Thoughts & Notes:

Prayer Requests:

Date:

Verse:

Thoughts & Notes:

Prayer Requests:

Date:

Verse:

Thoughts & Notes:

Prayer Requests:

Date:

Verse:

Thoughts & Notes:

Prayer Requests:

Date:

Verse:

Thoughts & Notes:

Prayer Requests:

Date:

Verse:

Thoughts & Notes:

Prayer Requests:

Date:

Verse:

Thoughts & Notes:

Prayer Requests:

Date:

Verse:

Thoughts & Notes:

Prayer Requests:

Date:

Verse:

Thoughts & Notes:

Prayer Requests:

Date:

Verse:

Thoughts & Notes:

Prayer Requests:

Date:

Verse:

Thoughts & Notes:

Prayer Requests:

Date:

Verse:

Thoughts & Notes:

Prayer Requests:

Date:

Verse:

Thoughts & Notes:

Prayer Requests:

Date:

Verse:

Thoughts & Notes:

Prayer Requests:

Date:

Verse:

Thoughts & Notes:

Prayer Requests:

Date:

Verse:

Thoughts & Notes:

Prayer Requests:

Date:

Verse:

Thoughts & Notes:

Prayer Requests:

Date:

Verse:

Thoughts & Notes:

Prayer Requests:

Date:

Verse:

Thoughts & Notes:

Prayer Requests:

Date:

Verse:

Thoughts & Notes:

Prayer Requests:

Date:

Verse:

Thoughts & Notes:

Prayer Requests:

Date:

Verse:

Thoughts & Notes:

Prayer Requests:

Date:

Verse:

Thoughts & Notes:

Prayer Requests:

Date:

Verse:

Thoughts & Notes:

Prayer Requests:

Date:

Verse:

Thoughts & Notes:

Prayer Requests:

Date:

Verse:

Thoughts & Notes:

Prayer Requests:

Date:

Verse:

Thoughts & Notes:

Prayer Requests:

Date:

Verse:

Thoughts & Notes:

Prayer Requests:

Date:

Verse:

Thoughts & Notes:

Prayer Requests:

Date:

Verse:

Thoughts & Notes:

Prayer Requests:

Date:

Verse:

Thoughts & Notes:

Prayer Requests:

Date:

Verse:

Thoughts & Notes:

Prayer Requests:

Date:

Verse:

Thoughts & Notes:

Prayer Requests:

Date:

Verse:

Thoughts & Notes:

Prayer Requests:

Date:

Verse:

Thoughts & Notes:

Prayer Requests:

Date:

Verse:

Thoughts & Notes:

Prayer Requests:

Date:

Verse:

Thoughts & Notes:

Prayer Requests:

Date:

Verse:

Thoughts & Notes:

Prayer Requests:

Date:

Verse:

Thoughts & Notes:

Prayer Requests:

Date:

Verse:

Thoughts & Notes:

Prayer Requests:

Date:

Verse:

Thoughts & Notes:

Prayer Requests:

Date:

Verse:

Thoughts & Notes:

Prayer Requests:

Date:

Verse:

Thoughts & Notes:

Prayer Requests:

Date:

Verse:

Thoughts & Notes:

Prayer Requests:

Date:

Verse:

Thoughts & Notes:

Prayer Requests:

Date:

Verse:

Thoughts & Notes:

Prayer Requests:

Date:

Verse:

Thoughts & Notes:

Prayer Requests:

Date:

Verse:

Thoughts & Notes:

Prayer Requests:

Date:

Verse:

Thoughts & Notes:

Prayer Requests:

Date:

Verse:

Thoughts & Notes:

Prayer Requests:

Date:

Verse:

Thoughts & Notes:

Prayer Requests:

Date:

Verse:

Thoughts & Notes:

Prayer Requests:

Date:

Verse:

Thoughts & Notes:

Prayer Requests:

Date:

Verse:

Thoughts & Notes:

Prayer Requests:

Date:

Verse:

Thoughts & Notes:

Prayer Requests:

Date:

Verse:

Thoughts & Notes:

Prayer Requests:

Date:

Verse:

Thoughts & Notes:

Prayer Requests:

Date:

Verse:

Thoughts & Notes:

Prayer Requests:

Date:

Verse:

Thoughts & Notes:

Prayer Requests:

Date:

Verse:

Thoughts & Notes:

Prayer Requests:

Date:

Verse:

Thoughts & Notes:

Prayer Requests:

Date:

Verse:

Thoughts & Notes:

Prayer Requests:

Date:

Verse:

Thoughts & Notes:

Prayer Requests:

Date:

Verse:

Thoughts & Notes:

Prayer Requests:

Date:

Verse:

Thoughts & Notes:

Prayer Requests:

Date:

Verse:

Thoughts & Notes:

Prayer Requests:

Date:

Verse:

Thoughts & Notes:

Prayer Requests:

Date:

Verse:

Thoughts & Notes:

Prayer Requests:

Date:

Verse:

Thoughts & Notes:

Prayer Requests:

Date:

Verse:

Thoughts & Notes:

Prayer Requests:

Date:

Verse:

Thoughts & Notes:

Prayer Requests:

Date:

Verse:

Thoughts & Notes:

Prayer Requests:

Date:

Verse:

Thoughts & Notes:

Prayer Requests:

Date:

Verse:

Thoughts & Notes:

Prayer Requests:

Date:

Verse:

Thoughts & Notes:

Prayer Requests:

Date:

Verse:

Thoughts & Notes:

Prayer Requests:

Date:

Verse:

Thoughts & Notes:

Prayer Requests:

Date:

Verse:

Thoughts & Notes:

Prayer Requests:

Date:

Verse:

Thoughts & Notes:

Prayer Requests:

Date:

Verse:

Thoughts & Notes:

Prayer Requests:

Date:

Verse:

Thoughts & Notes:

Prayer Requests:

Date:

Verse:

Thoughts & Notes:

Prayer Requests:

Date:

Verse:

Thoughts & Notes:

Prayer Requests:

Date:

Verse:

Thoughts & Notes:

Prayer Requests:

Date:

Verse:

Thoughts & Notes:

Prayer Requests:

Date:

Verse:

Thoughts & Notes:

Prayer Requests:

Date:

Verse:

Thoughts & Notes:

Prayer Requests:

Date:

Verse:

Thoughts & Notes:

Prayer Requests:

Date:

Verse:

Thoughts & Notes:

Prayer Requests:

Date:

Verse:

Thoughts & Notes:

Prayer Requests:

Date:

Verse:

Thoughts & Notes:

Prayer Requests:

Date:

Verse:

Thoughts & Notes:

Prayer Requests:

Date:

Verse:

Thoughts & Notes:

Prayer Requests:

Date:

Verse:

Thoughts & Notes:

Prayer Requests:

Date:

Verse:

Thoughts & Notes:

Prayer Requests:

Date:

Verse:

Thoughts & Notes:

Prayer Requests:

Date:

Verse:

Thoughts & Notes:

Prayer Requests:

Date:

Verse:

Thoughts & Notes:

Prayer Requests:

Made in the USA
Middletown, DE
08 November 2018